THE CHURCH AND ITS
TEACHING TODAY

THE MACMILLAN COMPANY
NEW YORK · BOSTON · CHICAGO · DALLAS
ATLANTA · SAN FRANCISCO

MACMILLAN & CO., Limited
LONDON · BOMBAY · CALCUTTA
MELBOURNE

THE MACMILLAN COMPANY
OF CANADA, Limited
TORONTO

THE CHURCH AND ITS TEACHING TODAY

Being the William Belden Noble Lectures delivered in the Memorial Church, Harvard University, on December 17 and 18, 1935

By WILLIAM TEMPLE
Archbishop of York

NEW YORK
THE MACMILLAN COMPANY
1936

Copyright, 1936, by
WILLIAM TEMPLE

Set up and printed. Published April, 1936.

SET UP BY BROWN BROTHERS LINOTYPERS
PRINTED IN THE UNITED STATES OF AMERICA
BY THE FERRIS PRINTING COMPANY

THE WILLIAM BELDEN NOBLE LECTURES

Terms Proposed by the Founder and Accepted by the
President and Fellows of Harvard College

The foundation having been established in memory
of William Belden Noble shall bear his name and be
known as The William Belden Noble Lectures.

The appointment of Lecturers upon this foundation
is committed to the President and Fellows of Harvard
College, hereinafter designated as the Corporation.

The Lectures shall be delivered annually at such
time and place as the Corporation shall appoint. . . .

The object of the Founder of the Lectures is to
continue the mission of her husband, whose supreme
desire was to extend the influence of Jesus as "the Way,
the Truth, and the Life," and to illustrate and enforce
the words of Jesus,—"I am come that they might have
life and that they might have it more abundantly." The
Founder has in view the presentation of the personality
of Jesus, as given in the New Testament, or unfolded
in the history of the Christian Church, or illustrated
in the inward experience of His followers, or as the
inspiration to Christian Missions for the conversion of
the world. . . . It is the desire of the Founder that the
Lecturer for each year shall be himself animated by
the further motive which inspires this foundation,—the

hope of arousing in young men, and primarily in the students of Harvard University, the joy of service for Christ and humanity, especially in the ministry of the Christian Church. The scope of the Lectures is believed to be as wide as the highest interests of humanity. With this end in view—the perfection of the spiritual man, and the consecration, by the spirit of Jesus, of every department of human character, thought, or activity— the Lecturer will choose his subject.

FOREWORD

THE William Belden Noble Lectures at Harvard were established in 1898 by a gift from Nannie Yulee Noble in memory of her husband, William Belden Noble, A.B., 1885. The stated object of the founder was "to continue the mission of her husband, whose supreme desire was to extend the influence of Jesus as 'the Way, the Truth, and the Life' and to illustrate and enforce the words of Jesus—'I am come that they might have life and that they might have it more abundantly.'" The founder hoped that the lectures would arouse "in young men, and primarily in the students of Harvard University, the joy of service for Christ and humanity, especially in the ministry of the Christian Church."

Twenty-three series of lectures have been given on this foundation prior to the academic year 1935-36. The lecturers have all been men of distinction. Francis Greenwood Peabody, Henry Van Dyke, William DeWitt Hyde, George Herbert Palmer, Charles Cuthbert Hall, Henry Churchill King, Wilfred T. Grenfell, Theodore Roosevelt, John Kelman, Shailer Mathews, Rufus Jones, G. A. Johnston Ross, Principal Selbie, have all stood before us in this connection.

Of the donor's own communion Professor A. G. V. Allen, the Rt. Rev. Henry Potter, the Rt. Rev. Charles H. Brent, the Rev. Roland Cotton Smith, the Rev. Charles Wood have shared in the discharge of the trust. More particularly Harvard has used the Noble Lectures as an occasion to bring to Cambridge devout and scholarly members of the Church of England, thinking that such use of the foundation would be acceptable to Mrs. Noble. The first of these English visitors was the Very Rev. Wm. Henry Freemantle, Dean of Ripon. He was followed, after a period of five years by the Rt. Rev. William Boyd Carpenter, Bishop of Ripon. In 1910 the Rev. John Neville Figgis was here. In the last decade we have had as our English guests in this connection, the Rt. Rev. Arthur C. Headlam, the Rev. H. D. A. Major, Canon Charles E. Raven, and the Very Rev. W. R. Matthews.

These Anglican lecturers have done much to further the aims of the donor and have with one consent addressed themselves directly to the theme prescribed. The resulting volumes have become part of the permanent religious literature of our day.

The academic year 1935-36 brought to the William Belden Noble lectureship at Harvard one of its most distinguished holders, the Most Rev. William Temple, D.D., Archbishop of York. The Archbishop's coming and his presence, as lecturer, on two evenings at the University Church, gave to the lectureship a fresh dignity and appeal. In his person sound scholarship, wide experience, simple piety, and the dignity of an ancient and a high office are met with a deep concern for a genuinely catholic Christianity. The Archbishop of York is known through our world both as a serious thinker in the realms of academic theology and as a Christian statesman. As the presiding officer of the World Conference on Faith and Order he holds one of the most strategic positions in the Christian Church.

Happily, and in faithful conformity to the suggested subject for the lectures, he spoke to the two main themes which most concern Christians of all sorts and conditions today; the nature of the Church, and the relation of Christian faith to modern thought. The two lectures were memorable occasions, and it is a happy thing that spoken words heard with such interest at the time of their delivery should now be made accessible in this form to that wider audience intended and anticipated by the provision that the Noble Lectures shall appear in print following their delivery.

W. L. SPERRY.

Harvard University,
Cambridge, Mass.,
February, 1936.

CONTENTS

THE CHURCH AND ITS
TEACHING TODAY

I

THE NATURE AND TASK OF THE CHRISTIAN CHURCH

I MUST begin what I have to say by expressing my very sincere gratitude to this great University for the honor it has done me in inviting me to deliver these two lectures upon this illustrious Foundation, and so to take my place in the list of those most distinguished men who have lectured upon that Foundation in the past.

It has seemed to me that it might be valuable at this time if we should consider these two topics, The Nature and Task of the Christian Church, and Christian Theology and Modern Thought or the Thought of Today.

It is evident that any treatment of those themes, which can be undertaken within the space of a single lecture each, can be only an outline. But there is some advantage about outline treatments of great subjects, because there is always a risk, where the treatment is more detailed, that the connection between the different parts of the subject will not become apparent. While every aspect is studied in detail, the attention is easily diverted from the unity which holds all those together, and in the result there is sometimes left a rather confused impression of argument concerning special points and very little general grasp of the idea which the lecturers have endeavored to set forth. Therefore we approach these subjects knowing that an outline is the utmost we can hope for, but trusting that the outline itself may be tolerably clear.

It is, of course, a familiar fact that when the physical presence of our Lord was withdrawn at the time of the Ascension, what remained in the world as the fruit of His sojourn here was not an organized society with constitution and rules; nor was it a book which He had written for the guidance of His disciples; but it was a group of disciples united to one another by their common allegiance to Him. It was a living fellowship. And that is not without connection with the whole nature of the work that He Himself had come to do.

Let us imagine what the situation would have been if He had in fact written a book that should contain His teachings for His followers. For all those who accepted His divine mission that book would have an absolute and completely binding authority. No doubt there would arise, especially as circumstances altered with the changing times, a need for interpretation, but so far as the meaning was ascertained, the authority would be complete and final. To exercise any freedom of judgment in relation to what was thus laid down would be almost equivalent to the setting up of the individual conscience against the utterance of incarnate God.

It is, therefore, of the very utmost importance to notice that our Lord did not take steps to provide for the fellowship of His disciples an exact record, in terms fixed by Himself, of the principles which were to guide them. But He left in the world a fellowship of people who had been His companions, who had come under His influence, who had begun to understand His work and person, who became His interpreters to the world. And for that reason there remains scope for freedom of intellectual activity in relation to the story of His life and teaching which would be impossible on the hypothesis that I have just mentioned.

Now, in the gospel story itself the chief conflict that arises and out of which the whole tragedy develops, is the conflict with the Pharisees, and that not with regard to any particular point of Pharisaic doctrine, but because of the whole character of that doctrine. The conflict is the conflict later summarized by St. Paul in the distinction between the letter which killeth and the spirit which giveth life. The Pharisees had developed a system of rules and regulations making almost a complete code for the conduct of life in the circumstances of their time. They professed to draw it from the divinely given law, though it is obvious that in large measure it arose out of the application of the spirit of that law rather than by logical inference from its precise terms. None the less, the code which they so developed was treated as being itself a precise direction for life, and it is over against that that our Lord develops not so much a doctrine as a glowing sense of dependence upon the Spirit, as the way of life for His own disciples. And this nowhere finds fuller expression than in the choice of a living fellowship rather than a written book, as that which should be the fruit of His earthly ministry.

Upon that fellowship, met together in the memory of the time that they had spent with Him, there came the sudden consciousness of new power urging them forth to proclaim the works of God as they had learned to understand those works, with a fire and an energy which communicated itself to all who heard them, so that from whatever country they came it seemed to them that they were hearing in their own tongues the wonderful works of God. And so, upon the day of Pentecost, the Christian Church as we know it was born.

To the Christians of that date it made no difference whether you should speak of them as being

Christians, disciples, having the Spirit of Christ, or being members of the Church. An isolated Christian would have seemed to them a thing quite inconceivable. They were a fellowship, so to speak, before they were anything else. They knew themselves to be a company of people in whom as a company the Holy Spirit was at work. And they knew that this company, which came to be called in course of time the Church, was animated by the Spirit of Christ so completely as to be in literal truth not only His Church but His organ of activity in the world—His Body.

But before developing that thought we must pause to ask how far this Church was new.

We speak easily and naturally of our Lord as the Founder of the Church. But is that the way in which He regarded Himself or in which His disciples regarded Him? Quite certainly not. There was in their minds a very great sense of novelty, no doubt, but it was not a new Church of which they were conscious, but rather the first attainment by the Church which already existed of the full sense of its own mission.

The word that was chosen to represent what we now call the Church—*ecclesia*—was a word which had been used to represent the assembly of the people of Israel. It is quite evident from St. Paul's Epistles that he regards the Christian Church as

continuous with the life of Israel. The great
phrases in the First Epistle of St. Peter, whereby
he described the special call and destiny of the
Church are, I think without exception, but certainly almost without exception, taken from various books of the Old Testament where they refer
to Israel. There can be no question at all that the
Church in the beginning of its Christian period
regarded itself as continuous with and indeed identical with that Church of the Old Covenant which
was known by the name of Israel.

It is perhaps worth while to point to some other
indications of this in the minds of the first disciples.
For example, there is the sense that it was necessary
to fill the place of Judas Iscariot in the number of
the twelve Apostles. The significance of the number twelve, thus carefully safeguarded is, of course,
that it is the number of the twelve patriarchs; and
the Church as it enters on its new career must
reproduce the characteristics of the old Church in
having at its head twelve foundation leaders. And
in the Book of the Revelation we find that in the
Holy City the names upon the gates of the city
were the names of the twelve Patriarchs, while the
names on the foundations are the names of the
twelve Apostles.

The association of the two Twelves, the Patriarchs and the Apostles, is plainly very prominent

in the mind of the early Church. And in the vision which opens the series of visions in that book, after the conclusion of the letter to the Seven Churches, the Church of all the ages is represented by four and twenty elders, because four and twenty is the sum of the Apostles and the Patriarchs together.

So then our minds are pressed back to consider what was the nature and calling of that Church of the Old Covenant which finds its fulfilment in the Church of the New Testament. And keeping to the outline treatment, which is all that we are following here, we may give a sketch of that history as follows: From before the dawn of human history there was, according to the Bible record, a community conscious of a divine commission to be witness to the divine truth on behalf of the world. Let us pause for a moment to notice how closely this doctrine of the divinely commissioned community coheres with our modern and undoubtedly more accurate understanding of human nature as in its profoundest essence social.

In the period when men thought of human souls as isolated atoms, affecting one another, no doubt, but in the last resort to be understood as each entirely the ground of its own activities, it was natural that heaven itself should be conceived in a purely individualistic fashion. But to a great extent our religious tradition has survived the shock that has really been administered to it in this respect by the developments alike of psychology and of the study of man's social habits; from that study we have come to learn that to a degree far greater than our fathers and our grandfathers were ready to allow, we actually constitute one another.

Undoubtedly there must be some novel and original element contributed by each individual to the scheme of things which he does not derive entirely from outside himself. That is true of every particular item into which the continual experience may be analyzed; whether you are thinking of a human soul or of a grain of sand, there is something about it which is itself alone, not derived from outside. For if you suppose that anything whatever is entirely constituted by its external relations and that this is really the law of being, then you can never get the process started.

Stark determinism is always stark nonsense; and the objection to it is not so much that it is immoral as that it is silly: because what it says is that A is A because of B and C, and B is B because of A and C, and C is C because of A and B. Then how does the process ever begin? Of course, it is true that in being A and B and C as we know them, they contain the product of their mutual interaction. But there must have been something, let us say alpha and beta and gamma, which were such as in this interaction with the rest to become the A and B and C that we know.

Stark determinism, if you try to think it through, presents you with the alarming spectacle of nothing whatever differentiating itself in this variegated universe by the interaction of its non-existent parts. That is not an intelligent scheme of thought.

There must be something there. And that will become of great importance when we consider—not in these lectures—the meaning both of moral and of spiritual freedom. But once that is granted, then we have to recognize how profoundly A and B and C have influenced one another in becoming what we know of them. We are the things we are because of the society in which we live and which we constitute. A purely individual salvation seems very sharply to conflict with any such suggestion.

The biblical picture of salvation through incorporation into a community entrusted with the knowledge of divine truth fits far more closely with the modern understanding of mankind. And it is, I am sure, no accident that, certainly in the country from which I come, and as I have been two or three times assured in this country also, the minds of students who are seriously considering the Christian faith at all, are becoming more and more occupied with the doctrine of the Church. It is bound

to be so as the knowledge of the social principle and
its place in our constitution become more complete
and more pervasive of our thought.

We look back, then, first to this community
which emerges from the mists where history, myth
and legend are all one, beginning with the record
of the call of Abraham, whether that represents the
movement of an individual who became himself
the founder of this community, or whether, as some
scholars would have us suppose, it really represents
the movement of a whole tribe. In the second case,
the contention which I have been advancing re-
ceives more emphasis. This community is, at first,
conscious of itself mainly as having a special relationship to God, whom it knows first as God Al-
mighty and later, after the revelation to Moses on
Mount Sinai, by the name of Jehovah or Yahweh.
And from that second stage, if not before,—but indeed the principle is implicit in the story of Abraham—the relation between God and His people is
that of a covenant which is a moral relationship.
No doubt this was not always kept in mind. Jeph-
thah is represented as regarding the relationship
between Moab and Chemosh as being identical to
that between Israel and Yahweh. Though that may
have been in the minds of the quite early Israelites
of the time of the Conquest, it is never accepted by
the editors of the books of the Old Testament as

we have them; and there was an increasing consciousness, increasing until it became possessed of the entire field, that the relationship between God and His people is moral. That is to say that God has chosen them by an act of favor, to which they are called upon to respond by loyalty and obedience. Moreover, along with this moral relationship, God is known first and foremost as Righteous Will, active in the world and active always in righteousness, so that the way of serving Him is not first by any ceremonial but by obedience of life.

Then as history advances and the prophets begin to enter more profoundly into the understanding of what it is that the righteous God claims of His people, it becomes apparent that the people as a whole will be incapable of responding to that claim. There arises the doctrine of the Remnant. Only in the few who are able to make a complete and thorough response to the demand of God will the purpose of God find fulfilment—not in the people as a whole but in the Remnant. And in the Second Isaiah the proposition is set forth that even the Remnant—if by that is meant any considerable number of persons—will fail in completeness of obedience, and in its place appears the Suffering Servant upon whom the Lord lays the iniquity of us all. The Servant as first introduced is perhaps the whole people of Israel. As the prophecy develops the name stands for the Remnant. At last it is a solitary Figure.

And so it happened in the supreme moment when the call of God demanded the completeness of absolute sacrifice. He who could make the answer stood alone. All the disciples forsook Him and fled, and Christ went out alone bearing His cross. In that moment the whole destiny of Israel was concentrated in Him. In Him the Church of the Old Covenant finds its fulfilment, and then, recon-stituted in Him, starts upon its new career. Freed now from national limitations, the entry into it is no longer either by birth into a particular nation or by naturalization as a citizen of it, but by incorpora-tion into the Body of the Messiah, something which is altogether beyond the capacity of the human will and can be effected only by the Holy Spirit.

The Holy Spirit is Himself first and foremost that power of which the infant Christian Church became conscious on the day of Pentecost. But it is known by the members of that Church as the power that arises in their hearts in answer to the love of God objectively displayed in the person of Jesus Christ. And the distinction—or at least the primary distinction—for our experience and thought be-tween the second and third Persons in the Christian Trinity, is the distinction between objective revelation and the response which it calls forth, both being activities of God.

And so the new Israel, the reconstituted Church, becomes in principle an all-inclusive fellowship. Nothing can keep men out of it except their failure to hear and answer the call of the love of God, what St. Paul speaks of as "the call upwards which God gives in Christ Jesus."

And so it is described in many figures, but conspicuously as the Body and the Bride of Christ. It has become traditional to use those two expressions as referring to the Church on earth and the Church in heaven. But if by the word "heaven" is there meant a condition only reached after bodily death, I see no ground in the New Testament for it at all.

The two phrases "Body of Christ" and "Bride of Christ" describe the calling of this society in two of its main aspects.

What is the task of this Church? Primarily to *be* itself and not to *do* anything at all. All that it does is secondary and expressive of what it is. And, first of all, its duty is to *be* in living actuality that thing, namely, the fellowship of those who have received the power of the Holy Spirit through the revelation of the love of God in Christ. It exists to be the redeemed community which worships as redeemed. And so far it may truly be said, if we know enough of what the word means, that worship is the business of its life. But because familiarity has blunted the edge of our apprehensions, it is necessary to pause a moment and to find what is meant by worship.

We think first, when we hear the word, of the various expressions of worship with which we are familiar, in the singing of psalms and hymns and the repetition of prayers, sometimes familiar and sometimes designed to express our needs at the moment; and perhaps we sometimes picture our own participation in the offering of that worship when it is rather apathetic and rather sluggish, and there has been about it nothing to suggest that in that moment we were coming nearer than in any other to the fulfilment of the destiny of man. But if this were all that worship means there would not be that deep concern which the Bible shows about the worship of false gods. If all we are going to do, so to speak, is to sing songs about them, I don't suppose it matters what we sing our songs about. Of course, the trouble is that every expression which we can devise of those things which lie deepest in our hearts, will always seem inadequate unless we are great artists in expression, poets or musicians, or at least, in the moment when we are offering our worship, are in sufficient sympathy with these great expressions to receive in our own hearts something of what was in the heart of the artist in the moment of composition. But what worship means is the submission of the whole being to the object of worship. It is the opening of the heart to receive the love of God; it is the subjection of conscience to be directed by Him; it is the declaration of need to be fulfilled by Him; it is the subjection of desire to be controlled by Him; and, as the result of all these together, it is the surrender of will to be used by Him. It is the total giving of self.

This we try to express through the various aspects of worship, in praise, petition, meditation and thanksgiving; and all of these are in themselves inadequate and will only mean what worship ought to mean if we ourselves feel the consummation of that meaning.

But it is evident that if this is what worship means, only the perfection alike of reality and of goodness can claim it; and to offer worship, in the true sense of worship, to anything other than the true God must be at least the most disastrous, if it is not—as it probably is—the most wicked, of all possible human activities.

The Church exists, first and foremost, to be the fellowship of those who worship God in Christ. It is, therefore, in this earth the representation of the life of heaven. Of course, it is easy for anyone who stands outside to look at us and say, "In that case we don't much want to go to heaven." Well, that is our own fault and not the fault of the call which the Church has received.

And if the Church once loses this mark, if it ceases to be first and foremost the community which, conscious of its redemption, worships its Redeemer, it loses what really distinguishes it from the other agencies for the general betterment of human life and will become easily merged among them. In fact, if its only concern is with the betterment of life on earth, or if this becomes uppermost in its thoughts or in men's thought of it, it is always open to the criticism that it is making use of a very large amount of apparently unneeded apparatus.

It is only when we understand the Church as existing first and foremost to be a worshiping community that we begin to understand either its nature or its task.

And that, incidentally, is the real ground of public worship. The reason why we, who are members of the Church, should join in public worship and not be content to offer our own worship by ourselves is that in our Christian faith we are members of this community, that we have received our faith from it and maintain that faith within it, and that the community itself is a worshiping community. What will be left of the worshiping community if all the individual members desire to offer their worship apart and in isolation?—even though we do not raise the question which, in a pastoral interest one is bound to raise, whether in that case they continue to offer any worship at all? The ground of public worship is not that each individual as a separate entity may be worshiping but that there may be in the world the thing that the Church exists to be,—the redeemed and worshiping community.

But worship cannot be the whole of our activity here, because it is, in its own nature, a concentration upon the God who appoints us our duty in life, and part of our very duty to Him is that from time to time, and indeed for the greater part of our time, we should not be explicitly directing attention towards Him but devoting it with all our energy to the duty which He has given us to perform. The principle of the fourth Commandment is an eternal principle. There must be some of our time set apart for God, in detachment from all other interests whatever, because unless we have that time for concentrated contemplation of Him there is no hope that we shall do our work in the world as a duty to Him and out of loyalty to Him. But it is also true that for the greater part of our time, represented in six days of the week, we have our duty to do in the power and under the direction of that Spirit to whom at our moments of worship we specially open our hearts. If worship became the whole activity of life it would almost—and I think quite inevitably—become idolatrous worship; for the worship that we are to offer is worship of the God of love. And if we are opening our hearts to a God whose own nature is love, so that He enters in and takes possession of us, this must issue in activities of love. It is not possible for us who are children of God and members of His family to approach Him one by one in isolation or to enjoy a communion with Him which is possible to us alone. If it is to the true God that we are come, then first we recognize that the only right by which each of us calls Him Father is equally possessed by all the rest of mankind, and the prayer is addressed to Our Father, not simply as representing a number of people each of whom means "My Father," but as representing the Father of us all, to whom we come as members of His family and in the companionship of all His children.

And, more than that, because the divine power that comes upon us and into us in worship, if our hearts are truly given there, is the power of love, this must express itself towards the others, our fellow members in that family. And so the Church, when it is true to itself, becomes the agency through which the love of God is active in works of mercy and service in the world. And it is in this sense, I suppose, especially, that it is to be called the Body of Christ, as it is called the Bride of Christ when we think of it in its nature as the community that, having been redeemed, answers the love of Christ with responsive love. That love, taking possession of the community, makes this its organ for working in the world, to draw the whole of mankind into the fellowship of love which the Church itself exists to be.

What activities are open to it in this field? That, of course, will vary greatly according to the conditions of civilization in which the Church is set to do its task. In some conditions of life it must itself undertake directly, in its own name and as a corporate society, nearly all that is going to be done at all in ministering to those who are in need as, for example, in sickness; and in the mission areas of our Church today it may be found that there is no activity of mercy and social benefit except what is conducted by the Church itself.

But when the Christian principle has taken possession of men's minds sufficiently for the public authority of any nation or race to begin occupying this ground itself, it is probably wise that the Church should withdraw from a great deal of its activity and become rather the focus and source of inspiration, in the power of which the secular community undertakes activities which, without that Christian inspiration, would have been neglected.

More particularly, in a highly complex society it has to be recognized that any public action always involves questions of judgment concerning what is well designed to effect its object as well as the choice of the object that should be effected. We may, for example, be united in demanding that by some means or other in a Christian civilization grinding poverty should be abolished. But there is room for abundant difference of opinion among Christians on the question whether any particular proposal will have the effect of abolishing it. And we must be very careful not to commit the Church to any one policy in such a way as implies disloyalty to Christ in those who, while desiring to cooperate, think that policy unwise.

Consequently when the stage has been reached at which the public authority of any secular community accepts moral responsibility in relation to that community, the function of the Church becomes a proclamation of principles, the indication of features in the common life which seem to involve denial of those principles and an insistence that those who are responsible should think out and undertake the necessary steps to make the principles apply.

Then the question comes: For what in the end

is the Church working? Is it to hope for and expect a final consummation in this world at all? We are taught to pray that God's name may be hallowed and His kingdom come and His will be done in earth as it is in heaven. Does that represent some millennium of social perfection towards which the Church should strive and which it should expect to see established?

That we should strive to secure such response in the hearts of men to the love of God made known in Christ as will lead to a perfect relationship between them in all their dealings with one another, is surely not open to question. That is most indubitably a Christian duty. We are, in that sense, to work for and prepare for the coming of the kingdom of God on earth.

But that does not mean that we are to expect to see established some particular state of society which, when established, is going to remain just as it is for evermore or, at any rate, till the earth gets cold and life is impossible upon it; for so soon as any such society is established, either some new thought in the minds of men or some new scientific invention or some entirely fresh and unexpected temptation to self-aggrandizement will come upon that society and disturb the equilibrium established. It is simply not conceivable that in the conditions of this mortal life the need of praying that the kingdom of God shall come on earth and the need of working for its coming should be over. We must work for and prepare for the greatest fullness of God's authority in the world which earthly conditions make possible. But the consummation is not and cannot be here. To mention only one thing necessary to that consummation,—it must be a fellowship not only of those who are loyal at any one moment upon the face of the earth; it must be a fellowship of all the servants of Christ, all who have been loyal to God in every generation. And that fellowship in its quintessence is not possible under the conditions of earthly existence.

Consequently the hope of the Church is not finally set on anything that takes place here at all. It must work for the expression here of the love of God in the hearts of men. But it must work for that, not chiefly because it would be so desirable a thing to see, but chiefly because the love of God is at work within it and is bound to produce this fruit. Meanwhile its hope is set on the fulfilment in the world of the resurrection, which stands for a transformation and translation into a new order,—not merely the continuance of this but the coming of another in which many things are possible of accomplishment which, under the conditions of our life, are not possible at all.

And that again is not a source of weakness for

the work of the Church on earth, but rather a power; for what mankind needs first and foremost is not a sociological millennium but spiritual redemption. If we are to lift the world, as Archimedes knew long ago, we must find a point outside it to act as a fulcrum for our lever.

Those who stir the world and carry it forward are not those at any time whose whole attention is fastened upon it, but those who live by a power that belongs not only to this world but to the eternal realm; and they are the best citizens of their earthly state who join with St. Paul in the confession that their citizenship is in heaven.

II

CHRISTIAN THEOLOGY AND
MODERN THOUGHT

As I remarked yesterday, in the treatment of such subjects as I am attempting in these two lectures which I have been honored to give here, it is necessary to confine ourselves to an outline. And if that was true yesterday it is still more true today. Indeed there would not be space within one lecture for even an outline of both Christian Theology and Modern Thought, especially in view of the singularly indeterminate condition of the latter.

There have been ages in which there was some prevailing philosophy. In the period when the Church's classical theology was framed, Greek philosophy held the field. And while there was a somewhat sharp division between the Platonist and the more Aristotelian schools, the differences between these were small as compared with the difference which separates Greek philosophy as a whole from many other conceptions of the world— or the ways to think about it—which have held the allegiance of men in different times and places.

Broadly speaking there was a prevailing philosophy; and the task of Christian theology was to set forth the meaning and content of the revelation which Christians believed themselves to have received in the terms of that philosophy, so that they might commend it to the minds of their contemporaries and also, in the same act, bring it into relationship with the other interests of men.

There is not in our day any one prevailing type of philosophy. Modern thought is in a state of chaos. There are any number of philosophies presented to us for our acceptance, sharply differing from one another. And it would needs be a rather futile task to attempt to give any account of them in outline, even were my own reading sufficiently capacious. But there are certain marks about the modern philosophies which appear in almost all instances. They are rather qualities of temper than schemes of thought.

The first is an insistence upon verification in experience of all which is commended for acceptance. I cannot suppose that the modern mind can be charged with anything so foolish as an attempt to dispense altogether with authority, because it is obvious that if we dispense with authority we shall, in every generation, have to begin at the very beginning again and, for example, instead of learning the multiplication table, we shall require every student of mathematics to rediscover it. What would have happened to my own progress in arithmetic in that case I shudder to imagine.

Obviously we all rely, at the outset, upon authority, and anyone who denies that is speaking without reflection. But there have been periods when people were content to repose finally and conclusively upon authority, and raise no further questions when once the authority had been accepted. Even this ought not to be set in sharp contrast with reason as the basis of belief, because the acceptance of the authority is itself determined by reason. But one of the great troubles which has been bequeathed to us by the ages of persecution is the identification of authority with compulsion. The proper meaning of authority is, of course, in its own nature an appeal to reason not in respect of the particular propositions commended by the authority, but in respect of the right of the authority to commend the propositions.

As all other ages must, so our age must begin with accepting much on authority. But it is less prepared than most ages have been to rest there. It is determined to sift and to experiment, to demand that what is presented as truth, especially in the spiritual sphere, shall be verifiable by the tests of actual experience. This, I think, is partly due to the influence upon the mind of our time that is exerted by the natural sciences, as a result of their triumphant progress through the past several generations. Every hypothesis in science must be tested, and until it has been tested by experiment it remains in the realm of speculation. It is not to be regarded as established until experiment has provided for it a basis other than that of the thought of the mind which first framed it.

But that is not the only source of this demand. It is also made because our world is conscious, as many previous ages have not been, that it is confronted with a whole multitude of bewildering problems, and that what is offered as a revelation of God ought to provide some clue at least to the solution of these problems. And if it is not possible to show how what is offered on the basis of authority can, and even does, affect the conduct of life and assist in the solution of the perplexities which beset us, our generation is ready to set on one side what is thus offered. There is the first characteristic, as I think, of the thought of our time,—a stronger insistence than has been usual, at least in the religious field, upon verification in experience.

The second is a certain form of the doctrine of relativity, a tendency to let the mind dwell forever in comparisons between practices or beliefs which are partly similar and partly different. This, I think, is due to two causes observable in the history of thought not long before our time. One is the rise to its present status of what men mean by History. I think it is fair to say that until Gibbon wrote his great work on the *Decline and Fall of the Roman Empire,* there had been no attempt similarly to achieve in a single panorama a perspective of a whole past period as a single process. There had been chronicles of events that fell within the lifetime of the writer, such as were written in antiquity by Thucydides, in the Middle Ages by Froissart, or by Clarendon at the time of the English Civil War and Restoration. While, of course, it had existed on smaller scales, there had been no attempt on a similar scale to take an immense period in the history of mankind and set it forth as a continuous and coherent sequence which the mind, as it passed over the record, could hold in a single grasp.

As a result of the great development of History in this sense we have learned that to know the origin of anything is a large part of understanding it, and that we can only understand it as it is when we also understand how it has come to be. But there men have often been content to stop, failing to appreciate the corresponding fact, that as we only understand what it is through knowing what it has been, so we can only truly understand what it is by also knowing what it may be, on points upon which sure knowledge is beyond our reach. This tendency, of course, has received great encouragement from the popularization, chiefly by Charles Darwin, of the biological conception of Evolution. It is hardly necessary to remark that Darwin did not invent Evolution. The idea is present at least as far back as Aristotle. But Darwin gave it a new influence. Not that he was the first to apply it in biology, but he was the first to give it vivid expression and to support it with detailed evidence in such a way as to give it a grip upon the public mind. Whether or not there be any causal connection between them, that habit of thought in science coincided with the development of the historical sense in other departments, and together these two have introduced what I have called a concern for comparison with regard to whatever is being studied, which has largely obscured interest in any inquiry concerning absolute truth.

Thus, for example, in the field of religion, theology and metaphysics have alike retired comparatively into the background, while in the foreground there appears what should be called the comparative study of religions.

May I in passing beg of you to avoid speaking of the study of "comparative religions." There is no such thing as "comparative religion," though there are a great many people who are comparatively religious. But the beliefs and practices of those persons are not the subject of this study.

The interest of the comparative study of religion is to trace out differences and similarities, for example, between Christianity and Buddhism. And there it ends. That is its function. It is of absorbing interest to those whose minds are drawn that way at all. The interest is so absorbing that when men have worked out the comparison as far as it will go, they are liable to think that they have done all that can be asked of them concerning the religions that they have studied. But there remains, of course, the question, quite untouched by this inquiry, whether one or more of the religions studied is in itself a presentation of truth. And any comparative study will not help you more than a very little way towards estimating the truth of the two things that are compared.

This is equally true concerning the other science which has come into the field and strengthened this tendency. That is the still adolescent science of psychology, adolescent in the sense that it is still immature, still far from being wholly integrated. Regarded as an entity it is suffering badly from what it has itself taught us to call the disassociation of personality and, consequently, from a certain self-consciousness or self-assertion.

There is a great deal that we have learned from

it already and a great deal more that we are going to learn. However, the psychological student of religion very often fails to notice that he is avoiding the question whether the beliefs which he studies are true. This is just one department of the application of the historical method. The student finds a belief concerning God and he draws out a scheme of the way in which this may have arisen in the mind of him who holds it. But that has nothing in the whole wide world to do with the question whether or not it is true. The history of the belief is not a criterion of its truth in any way at all. And if the psychologist insists upon explaining my belief about God by reference to the way in which my nurse treated me in infancy, I must account for his belief about my belief by the way in which his nurse treated him in infancy. Presumably he supposes that what he says about my belief is the truth concerning it. But why should we suppose that there is truth only in the method of psychological inquiry and not in any other? Why should the history of its growth be supposed to discredit a theological belief and not a psychological? If the history of an idea is all that can ever be said either in explanation or justification of it, that is as true of psychological as of theological theories.

Now, let us fully admit that theology has much

to learn from the characteristics of modern thought about which I have spoken, and from the special inquiries which have been prevalent in recent times and have generated those tendencies. In particular there was, as it seems to me, far too little insistence in the past upon verification in experience, and again far too little recognition that even though a man be persuaded that in his own religious tradition he has found truth, there may be also truth and perhaps supplementary truth in other traditions than his.

For example, when we consider the task of theologians who are interested in the missionary activity of the Church and the presentation of the Christian faith in such a way as may commend it to the intelligence of the educated Indian or Chinese, it is certainly vain, as it is probably wrong, to approach the traditional beliefs of those people on the basis of a sharp distinction between true and false religion. It is not to be expected that they will give sympathetic attention until full appreciation has been shown for the spiritual treasures of which they are the heirs. And in so far as these modern methods of study have led us to enter more sympathetically into the religious outlook of those traditions different from our own, they have led to a deeper charity and have brought us nearer to a truly Christian spirit.

In the New Testament the balance of this distinction is most exactly given. It is enough perhaps
to quote the declaration in the Fourth Gospel concerning the coming of our Lord, that in that moment there was the true light, the light which
lighteth every man, coming into the world. Those
who had never heard of His special coming were
not for that reason to be regarded as in total dark-
ness. The light lightens *every* man. The aspiration
after a nobler life, the pricks of conscience, even in
the simplest and least developed civilizations, all
come from the same Spirit who expresses Himself
fully in Jesus Christ.

Our Lord is presented as the culmination of all
religious aspiration, the shining forth in its fullness
of the light which to some degree is present in
every soul. That was the conviction to which those
were led who were closest to the Lord Himself.
It was when lesser men had the task of upholding
the new tradition so initiated against all the pressures of the heathen world that there arose the
sharp distinction between true and false religion.
It is not the word "true" that a Christian will call
in question, but the word "false." Of course, if he
is a Christian he will still claim that his religion
is true; he will believe that there is much yet to
be learned concerning it, and that he has not yet
comprehended all the truth that it at least imper-

fectly contains. But he will not draw the inference that everything other than this is merely false. It is something less of the same truth. It may be so far short of the fullness of truth as, in practice, to have the effect of mere error. But a wise man is likely to start with the conviction that there is no faith which is being held by any very large body of people or by any sincerely reflecting people, which has not truth as its mainspring.

Now, in this welter of modern thought with which we are surrounded and of which I have described some of the quite general characteristics, is there any question on which it is of supreme importance, from the Christian standpoint, that a clear answer should be given? We shall not suppose that it is the task of the Christian theologian to go on saying in every generation what was said by all his predecessors. Indeed, he could not now do that without involving himself in great confusion, for it is the task of theology in this age as in the first age to relate as far as possible the revelation given in Christ to the way in which men's minds are moving, so as to commend it to them and relate it to their other interests.

The reason why theology always must be changing is that it represents a relationship between an unchanging Gospel and a changing world. If the Gospel itself were subject to variation, then it would at least be possible that the relation between it and the world could remain constant, because if two terms are changing the relationship between them may be the same. But if one is changing and the other is not, the relationship between them cannot remain the same. Where one is stationary and the other moves, that relationship must be itself a perpetually altering one. It is the faith of Christendom that in the Gospel there is given an unalterable revelation of the eternal God, not in the form of doctrinal propositions which once and for all have been drawn up for the acceptance of men of every age, but in the form of a Person and a human Life to which all the doctrinal formulations point us.

Let us perpetually remember that the object of our faith is not the creeds but is the God of whom the creeds speak, and they are a way of professing faith in Him.

Now, from our currents of modern thought theology today may profitably learn at least a far greater insistence upon verification in experience. It is a fair demand which is perpetually made of the Church, that it should stand the test which is proposed, "By their fruits ye shall know them." How far it is standing that test or how far it will stand that test in the future are subjects on which I shall say something before I close.

I think there can be no question that religious faith today is suffering from the excessive readiness of Christian people in the past to dwell upon the authority by which their faith is commended, without reference to the fruits in which it is exhibited. And we can learn much, in ways that I have already indicated, from the modern tendency in thought toward relativity, in the sense of refusing to see the difference between Christian and non-Christian as merely that between white and black, and to realize that God is always revealing Himself everywhere and that all aspirations towards goodness and beauty are a true following after Him.

But also theology must insist, as against the tendency to demand verification, that if that is true which it tries to commend, the verification in this world cannot be complete. It is only in eternity that experience will become adequate to faith. And we walk, therefore, to the end of human history on this earth, by faith and not by sight. Nor shall we regret this; for it is evident that if religious faith could once be so established as to be entirely immune from any kind of criticism on grounds of theory or practice, it would become the natural victim, so to speak, of common sense, and the spiritual value would be sapped out of it. To act upon a perfect certainty is a mark of common sense and prudence, but there is about it nothing heroic. And the heroic element which characterizes all the great ages of religion and all the great religious figures, depends upon the uncertainty, in a logical sense, of the faith by which these are upheld.

Again in our recognition of the element of comparison between Christianity and other religions, and of the relative truth that is present elsewhere than in the Gospel, we must not lose sight of the claim which is essential to the Christian faith, that in our Lord there has been given a revelation which for its own purpose is final. Let no one suppose that this claim of finality is incompatible with that doctrine of progress that we so much love. Whether we are wise to love it is another question. But if we are to make progress, the first condition is that our directions should be fixed. No doubt we should be open to new argument, and if it can be shown to us that the direction in which we move is in fact mistaken, we should be ready to start again. But we should recognize that any doubt thrown on the sense of direction in our movement is not helpful to progress, but, so far as it goes, inimical to it.

You may decide, for example, that you will walk ten miles a day, and perhaps tomorrow you will walk ten miles north; then you will sit down with your companions and say that it would be an exhibition of stagnant minds that you should go on in the same direction and, therefore, next day you will walk ten miles east. And so you do. And that evening you decide that you are not crabbed conservatives enamoured of an old tradition, that you like starting out on new ways, and tomorrow you will walk ten miles south. And again you decide, for fear of being regarded as hopelessly obscurantist, that you will walk ten miles west. At the end you will have walked forty miles; and if you have calculated your angles rightly you will be precisely where you started.

The primary condition for making progress is that you know which way to go. And what the Gospel claims to offer us is not the realization of heaven upon earth here and now, but the way by which we must go. It does not tell us even where we are to arrive but only how to go. The literalminded Thomas supposed that you could not know the way unless you knew where it was leading you, and that, of course, is normally the case when you rely upon signposts. So he said, "We know not whither Thou goest; how know we the way?" The answer is, "I am the way." The invitation is an invitation to follow that way in faith, trusting in Him who makes the claim that it will lead us to somewhere better than any destination we could have chosen for ourselves. It is the way of faith and not of knowledge, but it may be a way of well-grounded faith, and it is a way on which it is always possible to start from any point at which you stand.

There is then in this claim for finality, for an absoluteness in that sense, nothing incompatible with our hope for progress but rather a new ground for that hope; for here at least is a promise that if we follow on faithfully in the way which has been indicated to us, we shall reach our goal at last.

And so Christian theology must insist, against these tendencies in modern thought, that while it accepts them so far as they will carry it, it must always go beyond; it must always say that while experience can add its measure of vindication to our faith, the vindication will never be complete, and our faith cannot be what it ought to be unless it transcends the very possibility of such complete verification.

And over against the tendency to compare and to establish relationships, we must make up our minds whether or not we consider that in the Gospel there is given a direction by which we should march forward, if need be, in only a small company, leaving the world with many wise and good people on some other path but convinced that this is ours. We are dealing not only with what is relative but with a claim to something absolute.

And, if that is so, then we begin to see the

answer to the question that I put just now, whether
there is some one point at which a decisive stand
must be taken on the one side or the other of a
dividing line. And I believe that it is here. We
leave aside for this purpose the atheist or the complete agnostic. To approach them we must adopt
some other method. But we are dealing with those
who have some form of a belief in God.

The fundamental question, perhaps for all time,
but certainly I am convinced for ours, is the question concerning God, whether He is a static perfection of being or is a personal Will active in the
history of the world. The former is the prevailing
Greek and Hellenistic idea and also the Hindu
conception and, in some forms of Buddhism, the
Buddhist conception now. The latter is the biblical
belief. I believe that distinction is one which we
are bound to draw and concerning which we have
to make a choice. Mr. Edwyn Bevan on two or
three occasions has declared that the broad difference between the nations of the world is not between Eastern and Western, but between the
biblical and non-biblical traditions. He points out
that the condition of the Western world, at any
rate around the Mediterranean Sea, at the time of
our Lord's ministry, was very much like that of the
India with which we are familiar today. There was
a noble and exalted philosophy, spiritual in its

quality and making an appeal both to the most subtle intelligence and to the highest aspirations of men, and side by side with this there was a mass of degrading superstition and much that was evil in human life, against which the noble philosophy was completely powerless and almost entirely inactive. And this comes, he insists, from the conception of the ultimate principle towards which our minds are turned in worship and in meditation, because if God is only a static perfection of being, always complete within Himself and detached from the affairs of this world, then all that is left for us to do is to contemplate Him, and our service of Him will mainly consist of coming into touch with Him through our intellects.

But the Bible sets before us a God who is, first and foremost, righteous Will, and whose first demand of His servants is that they conform their wills to His purpose. He can be served only by righteousness of life. And that whole conception of righteousness of life, and that conduct is nine-tenths of life, on which Matthew Arnold used to insist, is possible, in the long run, only if it is believed that this is the judgment upon us of the ultimate Reality, and that this is the meaning of human life in the sight of God.

Now, apart from avowed atheism or agnosticism, there have been in recent years two main tend-

encies of thought claiming allegiance. One presents
God as a pervasive principle; perhaps it calls Him
a Spirit; but it refuses to attribute to Him any
particular activity. He is the ground of all things,
but has never taken specific action Himself. We
are to find Him wherever we look. And no doubt
the better representatives of this tendency of
thought would add that we should only find Him,
in most parts of our experience, so far as we see
these in their full context, and that it is only when
we have watched the working out of the whole
process that we can detect in it the revelation of
God.

But if we are left to do that then we are indeed
in a sorry plight. If that is the truth, we must make
the best of it, but it will be a poor best, for it is
easily apparent that we only see the full meaning
of anything whatever, on that view, when we see
it in the context of the whole system of reality
which we are quite incapable of grasping. Therefore, our comprehension of God will be nothing
more than a dim groping, with some assurance
from our own sense of value that God must be
more fully revealed at one point than in another.
But that sense of value, though we may have to go
by it—because it is the only one we have got—is of
doubtful validity. And if we are left with no
guidance but that which such a philosophy can

give us, we shall have little to help us in the critical decisions of life.

For myself I do not believe that that kind of vaguely spiritual interpretation of the world, which does not find its center in a fully personal and transcendent God, has any hope of surviving under the pressures of modern knowledge and thought in the direction of agnosticism. I believe that the one kind of spiritual interpretation that can survive is that which insists with the Bible that "the Lord sitteth above the waterflood and remaineth a king forever"; and that no survey of ordinary human experience will be of itself in the least degree adequate to disclose Him to us, but that, none the less, He may be known by us because He has taken action to reveal His nature.

I believe, in other words, that Lord Balfour was right when he insisted that the only kind of faith which is of real value is faith in a God who takes sides, not only a God who is on the whole more on the one side or the other, but who Himself takes sides by active choice, who has a purpose and is perpetually active in the world for the fulfilment of that purpose.

In other words, I am persuaded that the central problem of religion today is the problem of divine revelation. Has God acted with the deliberate purpose of making Himself known and with the effect of making Himself known to those whose minds and spirits were ready to receive His manifestation? That I believe to be the crucial point.

No doubt it is the fact that very many interpretations of the purely humanistic tradition come very close indeed to the best and wisest interpretations of the biblical tradition; but they are on two sides of a watershed, and the streams flow down to very different kinds of country. The two rivers, the Rhine and the Rhone, have their sources close together in the high Alps, and when you are at the source of one you are close to the source of the other, and also close to the summit of the watershed. Yet the waters of the one flow to the North Sea and the waters of the other flow to the Mediterranean. And I believe that so soon as we abandon the conviction that God is such as to be able to reveal Himself in a specific act, and that He has actually wrought such an act for His self-revelation, even though our interpretation of the other view may leave us very near to the summit of the watershed and close to those who accept the Christian tradition, so to speak, at its source, yet we have started upon that incline which leads out to the arid wastes of pantheism.

Now, I fully admit that if we do accept this conception of a divine revelation we must be able to interpret it as a philosophy; and that will involve a great deal. It will involve, I think, our saying that God is revealed everywhere, because unless everything is a revelation of Him it would seem that nothing can be, just because it is God of whose revelation we speak; for God, if the name means anything at all, means the source of all things. And, therefore, if He is revealed anywhere He must be revealed everywhere, as the worker is known by his work.

Moreover, in insisting that He is a personal and not only a pervasive principle, we must claim, if we are earnest with the word, that He is at all times active in making those delicate adjustments to varying circumstances, wherein the life of living personalities consists; in other words, we must challenge the scientific thinking of the world at its foundation and roundly deny its totally baseless dogma of uniformity.

We shall recognize that because God is reasonable "He also is wise," as Isaiah once remarked in some irony to his opponents. For the most part, He will maintain a regularity of action sufficient to form the basis of the moral conduct of life. If God were going to vary the behavior of nature every time that it would suit your convenience or mine, we should have no secure foundation on which to base the formation of our purposes, wherein the moral life consists. A substantially reliable degree

of uniformity is necessary to the moral purpose of
man, which is a part, if only a small part, of the
moral purpose of God. But we shall not say that He
has left nature as a closed system into which He
periodically intervenes from outside, but rather
that in all things He is active as a living person,
directing His action according to the infinite wis-
dom that guides the fulfilment of the eternal
purpose.

That this will involve a very substantial re-
thinking of a great deal which has been traditional
at least in recent Christian theology, as in much
philosophy based upon natural science, I do not
deny. But I feel quite sure that our choice lies between a view of life from which in the end God
will be excluded as being no longer a necessary
hypothesis—and it is inconceivable that He should
exist in an unwanted fashion—and the view that
He is fully and completely personal, holding the
whole universe in His detailed control.

And if we look at the matter in this way, then
I would further suggest as I conclude, that faith
will deliberately submit itself to three tests at
least.

The revelation to which it points and on which
it rests must make a direct appeal to the heart and
conscience. "The word was made flesh and we be-
held His glory." There must be that appeal which

draws out from at least the best qualified beholders the appreciation of what they witness as unveiled. All of this, of course, has been lately set forth with great power by Rudolph Otto in his book on *The Idea of the Holy*, and in his gift to our language of the new word "numinous." There must be a numinous quality about it, if it is to be regarded as revealed. It must be something to which our spirits bow down in awe.

Next there must be dynamic effectiveness. That is the appeal to the test of experience which the modern mind proposes. It must be something which produces fruits. And it is not only a fact, but a perfectly just criticism of much of our claim, that the fruits which we are showing are inadequate to the claim that we are making. If God was in Christ and the Church is the Body of Christ, there ought to be more to show than there is. And the answer we have to make is partly to accuse ourselves and say the fault lies in our unfaithfulness, and partly also to make the claim—which is worth something, though it is far less cogent than we should wish to advance,—that the greater part of the good work that is done in the world, apart from any motives of self-interest, is in fact done by Christians in the inspiration of their Christian faith.

Certainly in my country—and I expect you will find it the same here—if you ask who are those who are doing the day-to-day drudgery of social and philanthropic work, you will find that nine-tenths of them are Christians, acting in the inspiration of their Christian faith. There is far less done by Christians than ought to be done; but most of what is done at all is done by Christians.

And thirdly, there must be the test of philosophic adequacy:—I mean that, as we adopt the hypothesis that the supposed revelation is what is claimed for it, it helps us progressively to solve both the theoretical and the practical problems of life; not that it gives us a complete and satisfactory scheme so that we can say that now we understand the whole universe and nothing any longer bewilders us—if any man should say that, we should know that he must be wrong—but as we apply it to one tangle after another it enables us to pick the threads apart and see our way clear to knit them together again in a serviceable fabric.

It must act as a clue to the various problems of life, guiding us progressively forward. It is of course held by the school of Karl Barth that the revelation from God strikes into the world from without, that it remains completely alien from the world and that no philosophy can be made of it at all. With such a view I am persuaded that in the long run the Christian mind will have nothing to do, and I believe it will be right. But it seems to me we must claim—and, in view of work now being done in this arena, can claim without arrogance—that though we could never by philosophic activity alone have reached the thought which the revelation sets before us, yet when we accept that revelation we are able by its help to produce and offer to the world a philosophy more comprehensive, more coherent and, therefore, altogether more adequate, than any other that is in the field.